Copyright:

*All poems and thoughts in this small book are mine alone.
They belong to : Andrew Provan McIntyre.*

All photographs belong to the author.

*Published by:
A C Designs & Beloved Pet Portraits.*

No part of this book may be reproduced or used in any other way without the written request of the author.

(c) Andrew Mcintyre December 2019-11-20

Isbn: 978-0-244-23523-9

A Christmas tale: What If.....

(A druidic bard living in Rheged, visits the stone circle in the fells. He spots a bright new star in the heavens. It shines in the east. He is intrigued and fascinated by this new addition, and follows the star light)

Every night he stood in wonder, within the circle of stones,

stones put there by ancients past amid the hills of Rheged,

he studied stars constellations and how they moved around,

he knew them all , the ones he could see that is,

and where their positions should be.

the constellation of the Bear illumined his spirit life

nothing really changed within the cosmic dance.

he sighed this night as he did every night

at the sameness of it all.

Wait though what is this he sees,

a star brilliance outshining the rest

constant in its place, never moving always shining

for many days he watched its light and wondered

he felt a compulsion deep urging him to go.

one deep dark night he packed his bag

slung over shoulder with his staff in hand

he left his Cumbric home, alone he went

wandered his way through Albions plains

passing villages small and large

the great stones of the south he witnessed for himself.
across the sea settled in a leaky leather bound boat
Found his way through the fields of Gaul
shivered his weary bones across snow bound mountains tall.
in the land of the Magyar horsemen mavelled at their skill
inched his way through Alexanders land saw the Spartans shields
and on a ship leaving Athens port towards the desert plains.
Lands that he knew not except from travellers tales
he was as strange to them as they were to him.
Exotic tents flapped in warmish breeze
their beasts with large feet and grumbly noise
plodding across the sand he was bumped and jostled.
Eventually one dark star lit night,
a beam of light shone down,
onto a humble stable with thatched roof
he had found what he was looking for
inside a child lay his mother crooning lullabys
All instinctively knew his reason to be there,
he was a guest expected a place for him was saved.
He saw the wonders of this world things beyond compare
travelled to this place ,from the west he came.
Followed a star in the sky without knowledge
of where he was to go only in his heart he knew
with faith he travelled there.

A Snowflake Falls

The ground lay hard as iron, the sky a steely grey,

Nothing dared venture out in this frozen waste.

Buildings lay in crumbled ruin, shapeless and deformed,

Shrines of glass and concrete ,no one left to worship.

Cathedrals to looming greed now fallen back to the ground,

Masters of the universe a delusory self title given,

Now they are like us all masters to survive.

All hope was taken food generated to resist disease,

To save us all they religiously proclaimed,

Instead they poisoned mother earth ,

Infertile she spins in black cosmic glare.

Weapons built to destroy the watchers of light

Soon faded into the dark recesses of hate

Understanding replaced by hate killed by men in shade

Fearfull to show their face cowards behind the silk,

Some fled into hidden places to escape the impending tumult,

But they were found to atone for their deceit.

Fires in forests raged sending glory to its doom

All creatures on earth who dwelt ,sacrificed in the sun,

A desert grew where once was none,

They called it a heaven on earth as long as we succumbed.

Now we the remnant that are left to wander Old Edens paths,

Looking for our escape to enchanted gardens growing

Where children are safe to play and run once again to laugh.

Winter has come, never really left ,with no festive fun,

Its as cold as rock ,perma frost, without sun,

No Robin song, no geese a flying, no hens, French or otherwise,

And no partridge in a pear tree, the wise had gone,

All sermons now were preached, herbs had frozen to the land,

Corpses of the modern age lay mangled , broken forgotten.

One day a child ran excitedly to his tribe,

Its face aglow like a candle bright,

It pointed to the sky and everybody looked,

From out of the steely grey sky,

A tiny snowflake fell.

A Winter Tale.

Tis the tail of the year

when the earth lies in slumber

and the ground is cold and forbidding.

Leaves have fallen and left

the trees naked and bare.

with skeletal branches

scratching at the sky

in vain and desolation.

Animals have curled up

and entered a slumber

of peace and isolation

no need for food

or water to bathe in

Under the hedgerow

others still scrabble

pecking and boring

at the lifeless ground.

Berries exist on some

shrubs and flowers

past their summer splendour
and into winters hard grip
Grey clouds of unforgiving nature
lazily wander amid sun yellowing grey
watching and waiting
for his arrival...................................

Fire is a crackling
smoke rising to the roof
to dissipate into the air.
Huddled round to warm our toes
and keep icicles from our nose.
A is still all is quiet
as snow begins to lazily fall.
The land is covered with
snow white blanket
from smallest grass
to fir tree tall.
Deep within the forest
something begins to stir,
an air of expectation
grips at our senses
and hair stands on end.

it moves ever closer

our nerves at breaking point

whatever can it be

lurking there in the

dark of forest tree?....

From the depth of misty snowy

fir trees skeletal branches shivered

as if from some spectral plain

stood a giant stag that snorted

white he was from antler tip

down to his little white tail

impressive he was, proud and free

the king of stags,come to me.

Beside him their came a stirring

shaking snowflakes from his beard

an old man appeared with twinkling

in his eyes and snow on his head

He stood tall and straight

dressed in white fur and leather

and by his side attached to his belt

hung an axe fashioned from

finest and sharpest metal.

With intake of breath we pulled

closer to our fire

as if that would protect

us from his obvious ire.

As we sat rooted with fear

with a smile and nod.

they soon disappeared
our breath we exhaled
into clouds in the air
A gift we were given
no others had seen
and cherished forever
in hearts and our mind.

Christmas Somewhere.................

The snow lay deep in the little town,

As night fell over the quiet streets,

All was silent nothing moved,

Horses hooves muffled by winter straw,

Within the stables snug, where little birds,

Huddled in the wooden eaves keeping warm.

A hole on the outside wall,

Where in wrens huddled crowded and content.

Occasionally a mouse appeared in the straw,

Almost trampled beneath horses shuffling hooves.

Outside it began to snow again,

Flakes illumined by candle light glow,

Shining out from cottage warm,

Through glass frosted in patterns bright,

Folk so glad to be inside.

Sounds of laughter from the tavern came

Voices raised and raucause in celebratory mein.

Down by the river where the ragged folk dwell,

Trying hard to be jolly amid the cloying mud,

Not for them the sweet aroma of myrrh,

Nor of incense clouding out the awful smell.

But still with sour ale and bread,

Celebrate the Christ child born in stable stall,

And secretly lighting a new cut log,

To cast a light through the winter fog.

A raggedy form stumbles in the snow,

Smell of ale sour on his breath,

Lies in an alley hidden from view,

As snow settles wetly on his back,

Dreams fill his head of sugar plums sweet,

Hoping for a visit from old St Nick.

In the cold light of day at first light,

A bundle of rags lay solid and stiff,

Missed by the sleigh and reindeer swish,

No one was there to see him pass,

Some who did thought "Drunken old ass",

Walked on by on their way to church,

Singing carols to welcome their saviour on high,

While forgetting the poor ,left to die.

While in the ragged quarter WENT UP A CRY,

ANOTHER ONE LOST TO WINTERS SPEAR,

FILLING THOSE LEFT WITH REGRET AND FEAR.

St Nicholas left gifts for the important and rich,

Tis strange how we are taught that he knows,

Whther we have lived life either good or bad,

Yet the good will die in a winters swell,

While the bad can celebrate with turkey and wine,

And the poor fight for meat with the rich mans swine.

Let the light from your log shine on the path,

That carries you through woods deep and dark,

Hail fellow well met along the way,

Break bread and drink ale shared out for all,

And relish in fellowship with yin an aw.

The Dance of Jacomo Frostus

Twas the end of year when nights grow dark
And stars twinkle in midnight sky.
The earth was asleep and trees leaflessly slumbered,
Under the hedges sheltered small creatures and birds
While hedgehogs snuffled and dormice dreampt.
Softly it fell without fuss or trumpet,
Covering the ground with soft white blanket.
Stifling the sounds into still and quiet,
Laying on branches weighing them down,
Turning all the world white and brown.
'Tis then that he comes all a twinkle and shine,
With shining toes and dazzling clothes,
With an icicle dripping from his nose.
Unseen and unheard pirouetting and pose,
Leaping and bowing until all is froze.
Creatures shiver and hold close
As star like, snow glistens and glows
But by mornings light and winter dawn,
He has passed by and gone,
Leaving only, the sound of twinkling toes.

MIDNIGHT SUNRISE

Sun sets over the hill and illuminates the north,

ice shimmers and creaks,

wolves howl cuts the thin air.

Reindeer cocks his head and listens.

Doors are shut against the cold night

as fire light glints off the axe by the door.

The sun it shines at midnights bell

Those hardy souls who live in the north

Watch in awe as the sky erupts

In waves of yellow,green and blue

Like waves of celestial seas

Carrying silver serpents

Over the star strewn sea.

The midnight sun burns and swirls

Beyond the ken of mortal man.

No Snow Falling.

No snow falling tonight all is dark wet and dreich,
Stars cant be seen all hidden by low lying cloud,
Shepherds struggle market price for sheep is too low,
children born in squalor no stables left,
now turned to houses for privileged and rich.

Wise men are shunned gifts not from them,
Heavenly choirs silenced none can hear,
auld drunks in fake beards to earn a buck,
amid the yearly greed no one actually gives a f...
walk by them and laugh gifting profanities in love.

Peace on Earth, goodwill to ALL ,love in the mouth,
war,bigotry and hate in the heart.
Those fleeing wars are treated as dirt,
what happens to them one day may be us,
will we be as smart to look for help.

Crying out to God or Allah to save us ,
but ignoring when life is good and sweet,
what a surprise we will find out one day,
that a child who was born in the middle east,
was to transcend all and to unite us as one.

On a cold chill morning

On a cold chill morning as mist hung over the sea
wives and children wrapped against the cold
stood like wraiths of souls long passed.
The dragon prow cutting through the pale yellow dawn
oars slipping into the calm grey water like knives.
a horn echoed from fjords cliffs haunting and surreal,
sadness and joy mixed as one.
down the still waters leaving the village behind
beyond the safety of calm waters embrace
out west over the churning sea
in search of land new beyond the mist.
To return in joy with the Gods safe hand.

Twenty first century nativity.

On the twentieth floor of a high rise flat,

A new born baby cries by his mother's side

Her name was Marie with no where to bide,

No father came to chase the rats.

The child lay in an old pram with no wheels,

No warm cot as the hospital was full.

On this cold winter night stars shone down,

Bringing no comfort in their nightly bloom.

She had left her country of warming sand,

To keep her baby safe from invaders hand.

Her husband died saving them both,

Pushing them onto an unsafe boat.

After months of agonizing fearful travel,

Arriving at a place safe and free,

Kept as a prisoner within a shed,

She cried to heaven, God save me.

A gaggle of young children came to look,

Disturbed at Maries baby's awful plight,

Scampering off again into the night,

Shouting don't worry Marie it will work out right.

She smiled wanely as she weakly rocked the babe,

Three men came in finely dressed and laughing,

Sneering at her and her new born child,

She screamed at them to go leaving no gift,

As they shrugged and laughing went.

Lying back on a soiled pillow seeking some sleep,

Hearing the rats scrapping at her feet,

Again she screamed and kicked them away,

She knew they would be back another day.

Church bells faintly rang through the frosty mist,

a congregation in finery sang their carols,

would she be missed at the food bank door,

night drew on darkness deep and dire,

what she would give for a warming fire.

Threadbare clothes pulled tight to her skin,

Cuddling her babe as her tears splashed down,

Holding him close to generate heat,

Cold biting hard at his little feet.

A friend came in at near dawn,

carrying some food and a warming blanket.

As dawn fully rose all was quiet,

No sound was heard in the dereliction,

Of this unholy squaler and rubbish,

The weak sun shone through the broken glass,

Upon three figures holding each other fast,

No sound was heard no baby cries,

No one to miss them at the homeless fires.

© andrew .provan.mcintyre.7 january 2018.

When winter snow.

When winter snow begins to fall

And frost sugars the flakes

In my house warm and snug

A tree stands proud and tall.

Upon this tree no baubles hang

Or berries shiny and red

But little drops of dried in blood

Crystalised by winters touch.

No lights to twinkle in the dark

Or ornaments gaily painted

hung their once a man

leaving us a gift of love.

This tree it stands throughout time

Reminding us of sacrifice

Along with holly and its spikes

A crown made for a king.

An aura of frosty air

Surrounds the tree like gossamer veil

At its foot presents gather there

A gift of life for us to share.

Winter Solstice.

Worgleschnortzkopf lay snuggled warm and cosy his blankets up to his nose.
His fire burned low giving his little home in the old oak an orange glow
Looking out his window from under his blankets he watched stars twinkle
Now and then one would shoot in a white streak across the starry domain
He smiled to himself , a smile of contentment and happy repose.
Cupboards were full of winter provision collected while summer sun shone
Snow began to fall softly and slowly covering the woods with fine white dust
Jacomo Frostus began to dance leaving crystals behind like stars on earth
Worgle caught a glimpse of the jester of ice as he danced by his window
Leaving it covered in patterns of ice like spiders web frozen forever in time.

Woodland creatures huddled in dreys and nests hidden deep in branches
Wrens crammed together in holes in trees keeping each other warm
While winters cold began to bite and nip at feet and feathered wing
And Robin with head under wing in the centre of bramble thicket.
Sleeping soundly and safe protected from chill and harsh wind.
At dawns first glimpse yellow and bright snow and icickles
Decorating trees small and mighty

On this winters morn beginning new adventures for all in the woods.
Worgle slowly and deliberately rose from his bed yawning and stretching
From his head to his toes,placing logs on the fire pleasing sparks flew up
His kettle he filled with water to boil and mushrooms soon sizzled
In his old well used frying pan and with tatties and fruits he will soon break fast

Washing it down with tea made with nettles and herbs inner heating for him

Dressed in cap woollen and green, boots of soft leather and coat brown and worn

Stepped out his door and took in deep breathes of clean fresh air

Filling his lungs with the chill air ,bracing and refreshing waking his soul.

What a day to be here he thought to none but himself as always alone

He went about his garden brushing off snow from his plants and stones

He suddenly stopped as he heard twigs snap raised his head to look

An old man appeared no taller than himself with back bent double

Carrying his load of twigs and branches ready for the fire

At his own hearth and home , wherever that was.

He raised his old head and looked with watery eye towards Worgleschnortzkopf

Smiled and tried slowly to wave and went about his business crooked and slow

A pang of remorse swept through Worgles being and he rushed to help,

carried themto the old mans home not far from Worgles home in the oak.

Deep in the roots of an old birch bole he beckoned Worgle to follow

Down a dark hole ,dank and damp, where worms will dwell

Then to his surprise they came to a hall all golden and shiney

With stars dripping and running down the walls

Song fae and old heard in the air played on harps and lutes carved from wood ancient

and old, polished with bees wax to give a shine like unto gold.

Dancers there were all colourfully dressed

Made from silks of butterfly larvae, colours so bright

Tables laden with fruits and ales, ciders and wines from Honeysuckle juice pale and

thick, and of golden hue.

Hazlenuts, chestnuts and acorn stew, mushrooms in soup

Thick and hearty, salads of nettle and dandelion stalks with parsley and garlic

Nastursham petals and starflowers blue hue covered the tables

And scent filled the air of lavender and apple blossom

Worgleschnortzkopf stood with eyes wide in amazement

Women of fae and fair of face approached him with a smile full of grace

And danced with him long into the night while stars looked down

When at last he woke he was wrapped up in bed

Blankets pulled up under his nose head on pillow of duck down soft

Did he dream of last nights feast and dance with a woman so fair

As to inhabit his dreams long into the year?

At the foot of his bed hung a bag not of his

Looking into it a spied a glass globe which swirled and glowed from within

In it he saw golden light with star light dripping and fae music playing

Tables filled with all kinds of good fare a harp and lute plucking a tune

A womans smile warm and loving smiled at him from within the glass

With a wink and a scamper across a floor with flash of silver she was no more.

Solstice Eve

Hush my little ones – be snug and warm

Winter has come – time for sleep.

****

The sky is dark, stars twinkling bright

Looking below at a garden asleep,

Branches are bare except evergreens fronds,

In holes in old oak trunk

Wrapped up in moss, straw and dry grass,

Sleeps the winter through, little dormouse.

Wrens huddled together in roosting pocket

Robins head under wings safe from the chill,

Deep within holly bush crown

Blackbirds sleep , dream of the spring.

Songs of the thrush silenced for now

Finches and sparrows squabble in snow

Little footprints like some pattern drawn

Delicate as lace soon be gone.

Hedgehogs curled asleep warmed by dry leaf

Spikes keep them safe from marauding thief,

Stoats all white in new winter coat

Chase after hares round and round

Venturing out occasional badgers roam

Looking for worms grubs and things.

High in their dreys squirrels eye shut

Red and grey hide for the day

Owls silently hover mid flight

Looking for creatures

who venture out in the night.

****

The garden is quiet tonight in silence asleep

As Jack dances and spins frosty feet

A Dormouse wrapped warm in its nest

Within an old oak safe and secure.

While away in the distance a bell rings out.

****

Hush my babies----sleep safe and secure

Dream of the sun----and warm days to come

Years End.

The year it draws to a close ,

winter darkness slow and deep with stars a sparkle ,

to light the path, of unwary travellers caught without a home fire bright.

Travelling on roads unfamiliar and rocky, where holes appear to hinder

To catch those who sleep while still awake.

Open your eyes ,open your senses,

with discernment see what others cant.

Forgive those who walk blind to hazards unseen

who fall for the voice that seeks to deceive.

Let the scales fall from their eyes and see the truth for themselves eventually it comes

the dawning of light filling their senses with freedoms delight.

Tae a Sprout(Brussels that is).

Wee roon green cabbage in minature,what a stushie yer causin fowk to be I,Dae we like you?Or dae wi no?thats a question even auld Hawkins widnae know, Full of goodness like iron an things sae im tellt, bet theyve never the aftermath smelt, A childs worse horror at festive time, these slinky wee green things lookin like slime, always there at the side o the plate, nae trifle fur ye till that lots ate, this threat came out o the blue, but maw hoo can i eat summat the looks like glue.o wee green cabbage where ever yer grown be it ower the sea in Brussels toon,or in a flat field doon Lincoln way,Yer always there liked or no,but at christmas time yer there mair than snow.

CPSIA information can be obtained
at www.ICGtesting.com
Printed in the USA
LVHW081611220622
721875LV00015B/642